AF583733

Australian GEOGRAPHIC

Geography

Global Connections

MALAYSIA

32
MILLION
PEOPLE

INDONESIA

267
MILLION
PEOPLE

TIMOR-LESTE

1.3
MILLION
PEOPLE

AUSTRALIA

24.6
MILLION
PEOPLE

Australia's neighbours

UNLIKE MANY COUNTRIES, Australia does not share land borders with any other nations. But our island continent is situated close to Asia and the Pacific islands, with whom it shares important relationships. Australia is linked with its neighbours through trade, education and provision of foreign aid, as well as thriving tourism industries. Migration also plays a large role in shaping Australia's identity.

Did you know?

It takes nearly four times as long to fly from Darwin, Australia to Dili, Timor Leste as it does to fly from Sydney to Perth.

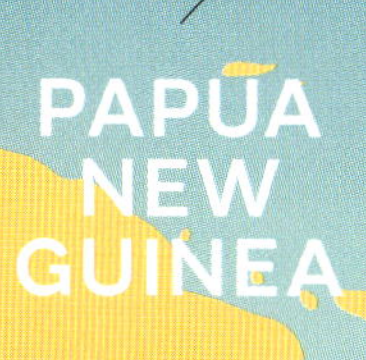

PAPUA NEW GUINEA

8.4 MILLION PEOPLE

SOLOMON ISLANDS

620,000 THOUSAND PEOPLE

198,000 THOUSAND PEOPLE

SAMOA

280,000 THOUSAND PEOPLE

VANUATU

FIJI

910,000 THOUSAND PEOPLE

TONGA

110,000 THOUSAND PEOPLE

NEW CALEDONIA

280,000 THOUSAND PEOPLE

4.75 MILLION PEOPLE

NEW ZEALAND

Australia's migrants

PEOPLE WHO LEAVE their home country to settle and live permanently in a different country are called migrants. When the Commonwealth of Australia was formed in 1901, immigration programs favoured applicants from certain countries and refused entry to others. Currently, Australia accepts a maximum of 190,000 migrants every year through its Migration Programme. In 2017–18, 162,417 people migrated to Australia. These people are selected based on a range of criteria, but never based on race or religion. Selection criteria include:

- ✓ Are they related to an Australian citizen or permanent resident?
- ✓ Do they have skills we need in Australia?
- ✓ What qualifications do they have?
- ✓ How old are they?
- ✓ How much money and business can they bring to Australia?
- ✓ Are they healthy? Do they have good character?

Did you know?

In 1945, at the end of World War II, Australians realised that they needed more citizens to defend their country and help develop their industries. So the government began encouraging more people from overseas to come and live in Australia.

Where do they settle?

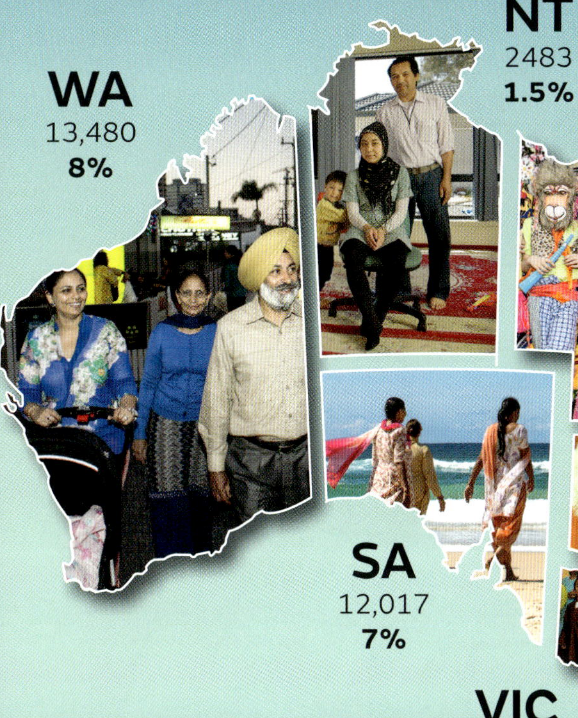

Where do they come from?

INDIA
33,310

CHINA
25,145

UNITED KINGDOM
13,654

PAKISTAN
6,235

PHILLIPINES
10,610

NEW ZEALAND
8,199

SKILL
111,008 68%
Most migrants have particular work skills that Australia needs, or are nominated by an Australian-based employer.

FAMILY
47,732 29%
People with partners, spouses, parents or dependent children who live in Australia can be accepted as migrants.

SPECIAL ELIGABILITY
236 0.1%
This category is for former permanent residents returning to Australia.

CHILDREN
3550 2%
There is no limit on the number of children who can apply for and receive visas.

HUMANITARIAN
16,250
Australia's humanitarian programme accepts refugees. Refugees are people who are forced to leave their home due to war, conflict or human rights abuses.

Australia's exports

AN EXPORT IS A product or service that is sent to another country to be sold. Australia exports a variety of goods and services, worth more than AU$386 billion in 2017. Most of our exports are minerals, such as iron and gold, and agricultural products such as wool and beef. The third-biggest export earner is education, with hundreds of thousands of international students paying to learn English or study at university in Australia. Tourism is another important service export for Australia.

KEY PARTNERS

China
$141 BILLON
(Including Hong Kong and Taiwan.) Iron, coal, wool, gold and copper.

Japan
$47 BILLION
Coal, iron, gas, copper and beef.

South Korea
$23 BILLION
Coal, iron, petrol, beef and sugar.

USA
$21 BILLION
Beef and other meat products, wine, and aircraft parts.

India
$20 BILLION
Coal, copper, vegetables and gold.

New Zealand
$14 BILLION
Chocolate, medicine, and computers.

Singapore
$12 BILLION
Gold, petrol, animal oils and fats and other aircraft parts.

UK
$12 BILLION
Gold, lead and wine.

Indonesia
$9 BILLION
Wheat, petrol, animals and coal.

Australia's imports

AN IMPORT IS A product or service that is brought from abroad into Australia to be sold. Australia's biggest import is actually Australian people paying to travel overseas. Australia also imports cars to drive and the petrol to power them. Altogether, Australia imports goods and services worth AU$376 billion.

TOP 5 EXPORTS

IN 2017

KEY PARTNERS

China
$67 BILLON
Telecommunications equipment, computers, clothes and furniture.

USA
$47 BILLION
Cars, aircrafts and parts, telecomunications and medical equipment.

South Korea
$32 BILLION
Petrol, ships and boats, cars, and household appliances.

Japan
$25 BILLION
Cars and other vehicles, petrol and gold.

Thailand
$17 BILLION
Cars and other vehicles, air conditioning, household appliances and gold.

Germany
$17 BILLION
Cars and other vehicles, medicines.

UK
$15 BILLION
Cars, medicine, alcohol and printed matter.

Singapore
$13 BILLION
Petrol, computers, and foodstuffs.

New Zealand
$13 BILLION
Food, gold, petrol, tobacco, alcohol and cheese.

Australia's favourite places

AUSTRALIANS LOVE TO visit other places and spend a lot of money travelling overseas. Some places are very popular among Australian holidaymakers.

1. New Zealand
2. Indonesia
3. USA
4. UK
5. Thailand
6. China
7. Singapore
8. Japan
9. India
10. Fiji

New Zealand

China

1 New Zealand

Nearly one and a half million people travelled to New Zealand in 2017. Some of these are probably New Zealanders who live in Australia visiting family at home. But New Zealand offers many experiences that Aussies love, such as skiing and bushwalking in the Southern Alps. Travelling to New Zealand is easy for most Australians because they are automatically granted a visa.

5 Thailand

Thailand is another South-East Asian country that attracts Australians, with tropical resorts, beaches and warm weather. More than half a million Australians visited Thailand in 2017.

6 China

More than half of the visitors to China from Australia are there for a holiday, though many people travel for work or family reunions. The proximity of the country is a strong pull for tourists, with many including prolonged stays as stops on international trips.

2 Bali, Indonesia

Bali, an island in Indonesia, has long been a preferred holiday destination for Australians. With beautiful beaches, comfortable resorts and affordable flights, it's an accessible spot for many Aussies seeking a tropical escape. More than 1.1 million Australians visited Indonesia in 2017.

Australia's tourists

MORE THAN 9 million people visit Australia every year. Tourism is an important part of Australia's economy, with the millions of visitors collectively spending more than $42 billion on their Aussie travels.

What do tourists come to see and do?

Wildlife – many tourists come to see Australia's iconic marsupials such as kangaroos and koalas.

Great Barrier Reef – the world's largest fringing reef, off the coast of northern Queensland, offers amazing opportunities to snorkel and dive with coral, sea turtles and tropical fish.

Visit iconic landmarks – tourists come to see Aussie icons, including man-made ones such as the Sydney Opera House, and natural ones such as Uluṟu in the Outback.

Experience Aboriginal culture – tourists visit many important Indigenous locations around Australia, as well as places like Indigenous art galleries.

Visit Australia's beaches – from city beaches such as Bondi Beach in Sydney, to wild expanses of white sand such as the Whitsundays in northern Queensland.

Work – Young people aged between 18–30 years old from certain countries can come to Australia on a working holiday visa, which allows them to work and travel in Australia for one year.

Education

INCREASING RATES OF EDUCATION generally lead to lower levels of poverty, and education gives people a great ability to lead healthy, productive lives. But not everyone has the opportunity to receive an education.

Access issues

Around the world, 61 million children are not enrolled in primary school, often because of conflict in the countries where they live. More than half of these children are girls, and about one-third have a disability.

Girls are more likely to be out of school compared to boys, especially those from poor families or those in conflict-affected regions. Helping girls to stay in school can have enormous health and economic benefits for them personally as well as more generally for their region.

Quality of education is also an issue, as millions of children cannot read and write despite going to school.

HOW AUSTRALIA HELPS EDUCATION IN THE ASIA-PACIFIC REGION

Australia helps countries in the Asia-Pacific region to improve the quality of education, and boost the number of children attending school. In the region, more than 17 million children do not attend school. But with Australia's assistance, 1.1 million more children were enrolled in 2015 and 2016. The government partners with organisations, experts and companies to achieve this. There is a particular focus on increasing access and opportunities for girls and children with disabilities.

Australia also supports the training of teachers. More than 135,000 teachers received training as a result of Australia's funding in 2015–16. For example, Australia helps women from ethnic minorities in Laos train as teachers, giving them a job opportunity close to home and providing positive role models for other young girls.

In 2018–19, Australia has dedicated more than $637 million to education across the Asia-Pacific.

TEACHER TRAINING

Did you know?

Indigenous Australian children have a significantly lower rate of school attendance than the rest of the population.

Australia Awards

The Department of Foreign Affairs and Trade (DFAT) offers over 3000 scholarships and courses to students from developing nations as part of its Australia Awards program. Students from the Pacific, Asia, Middle East and Africa receive scholarships to study at Australian universities, while some Australian students travel to study overseas. This creates links between Australia and her neighbours, and develops a network of future leaders. DFAT also funds fellowships to train professionals and leaders.

MORE THAN **135,000** teachers received training as a result of Australia's funding in 2015–16.

61 MILLION children are not enrolled in primary school, often because of conflict where they live.

Australia has dedicated over **$637 MILLION** to education across the Asia-Pacific.

Defence

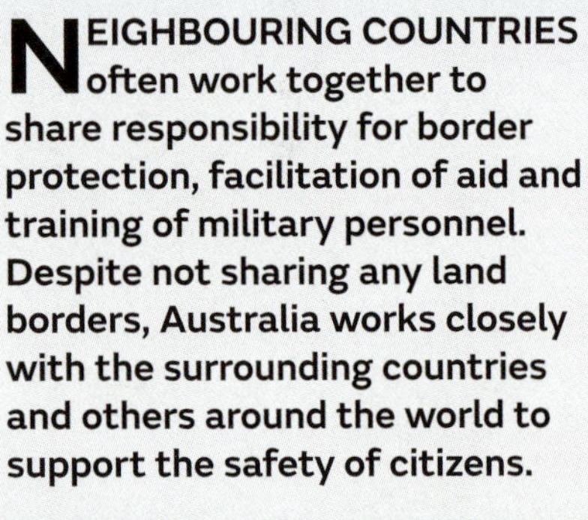

NEIGHBOURING COUNTRIES often work together to share responsibility for border protection, facilitation of aid and training of military personnel. Despite not sharing any land borders, Australia works closely with the surrounding countries and others around the world to support the safety of citizens.

The Australian Defence Force

The Australian Defence Force (ADF) consists of the Royal Australian Navy, Australian Army and Royal Australian Air Force. Combined, they employ more than 80,000 people. The ADF is administered by the government's Department of Defence. The ADF currently has forces deployed in the Middle East and in the Asia-Pacific region. ADF units patrol Australia's Exclusive Economic Zone (EEZ) – the ocean area that belongs to Australia – as well as parts of the South China Sea and south-west Pacific Ocean.

Joining forces

The ADF works with many different military forces from around the world. Some important allies include the United States, United Kingdom, Canada, New Zealand, Singapore and Malaysia. With these partners, the ADF participates in joint military exercises, shares intelligence and exchanges equipment or staff.

New Zealand, Singapore and the USA have small military units based in Australia.

PARTNERSHIPS INCLUDE:

- **Pacific Patrol Boat Program, with 22 boats operated by 12 Pacific countries.**
- Deploying ships and aircraft to patrol the waters of Pacific island countries.
- **Helping to safely remove explosive remnants left behind after World War II from Pacific island nations.**
- Supporting the development of the defence forces in Timor-Leste and Papua New Guinea.
- **Defending Nauru (in an informal agreement).**
- Operation Gateway: Australia supports Malaysia through providing ships for regular surveillance in the South China Sea.
- **Operation Augury: Australia helps the Philippines to develop counterterrorism tactics.**

A multicultural nation

SINCE EUROPEAN COLONISATION in 1788, people from many different parts of the world have immigrated to Australia and settled here, bringing their unique cultures, languages and cuisines with them. This makes Australia a multicultural nation, where people are allowed to freely express their cultural and religious identity.

Languages

1/5 OF AUSTRALIANS

speak a language other than English at home. Other languages spoken include Mandarin, Vietnamese, Italian, Arabic and Aboriginal languages.

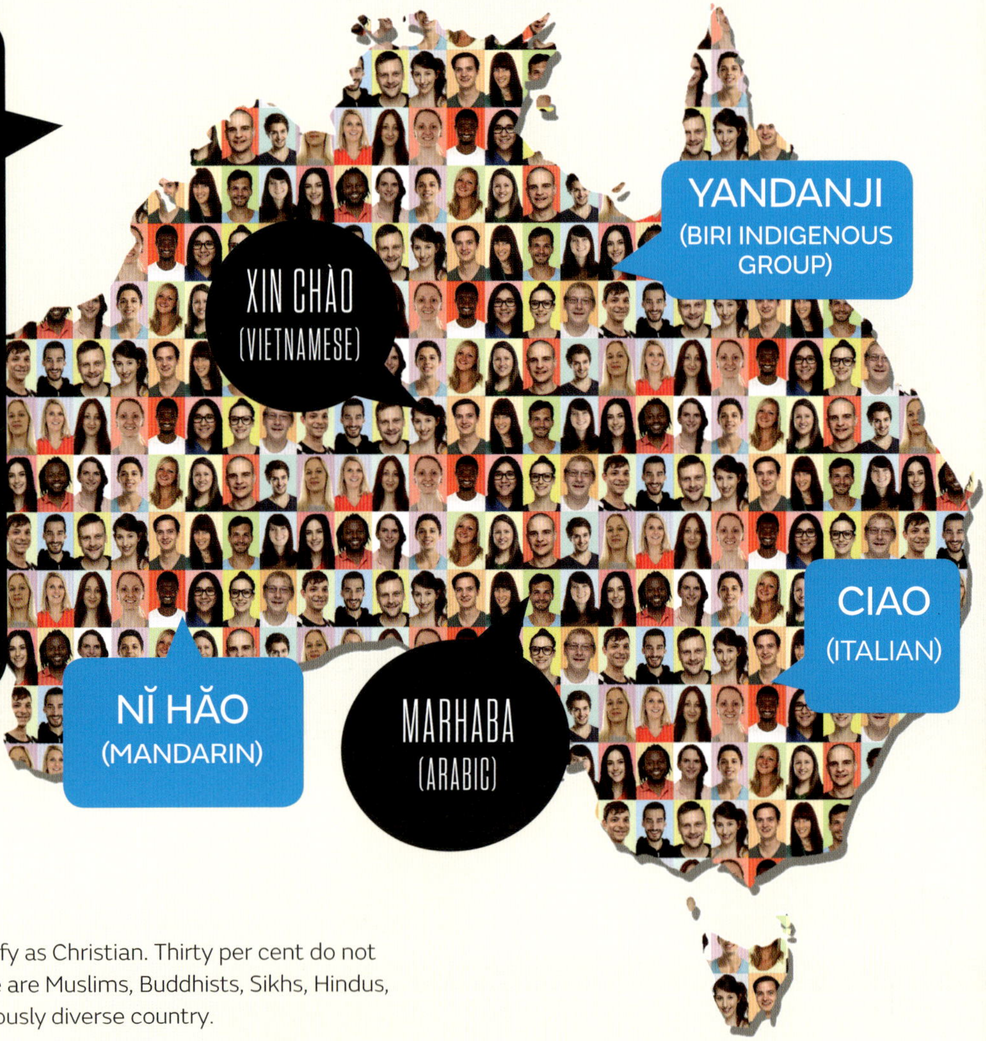

XIN CHÀO
(VIETNAMESE)

YANDANJI
(BIRI INDIGENOUS GROUP)

CIAO
(ITALIAN)

MARHABA
(ARABIC)

NǏ HǍO
(MANDARIN)

Religions

Just over half of Australians identify as Christian. Thirty per cent do not practise any religion. Other people are Muslims, Buddhists, Sikhs, Hindus, and Jews. Australia is a very religiously diverse country.

Multicultural Festival

Every February, Canberra hosts the National Multicultural Festival, which celebrates the diversity of cultures in Australia. The festival features more than 300 different food stalls and an array of dance and musical performances. Other cities around Australia also hold cultural festivals, including the Adelaide Multicultural Festival, pictured here.

Cultural places

Australia's multiculturalism is reflected in its places. Sydney is home to Australia's largest Chinatown, where you can find many Chinese restaurants, and street signs in both English and Mandarin.

The town of Cowra, in western New South Wales, has an association with Japan. During World War II, it was the site of th Cowra Prisoner of War Camp. In 1944, more than 1000 Japanese prisoners tried to escape from the camp and 231 were killed, as well as four Australian soldiers. To commemorate this traumatic event, Cowra has a large Japanese war cemetery and a traditional Japanese garden with cherry blossoms. As a town, they promote values of peace and acceptance.

Australia's foreign aid

Why give aid?

Giving aid to countries in need helps to make the region stable, strong, and prosperous. Aid helps people by alleviating poverty, improving health and education, and providing economic opportunities.

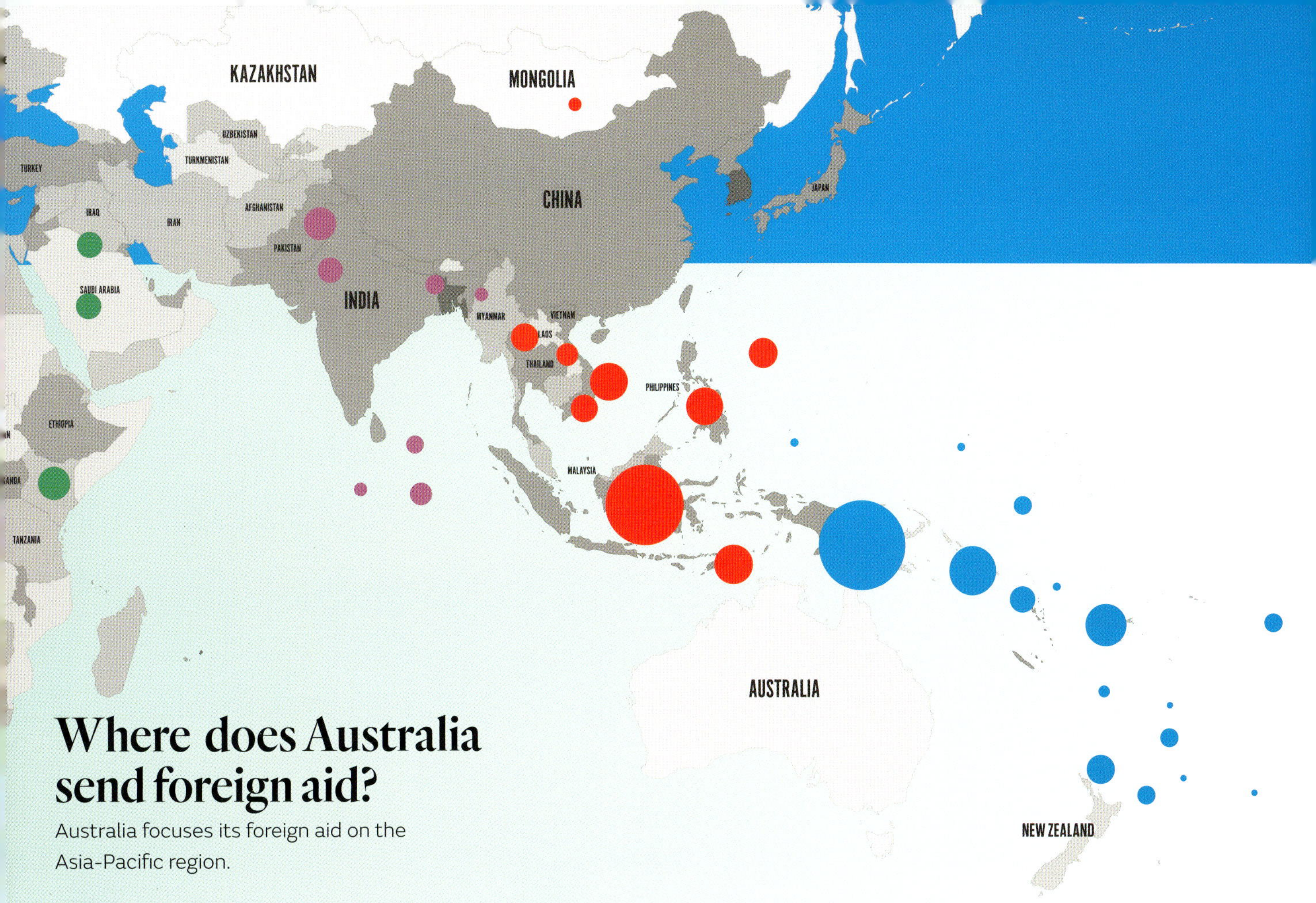

KAZAKHSTAN
MONGOLIA
UZBEKISTAN
TURKMENISTAN
TURKEY
IRAQ
IRAN
AFGHANISTAN
CHINA
JAPAN
PAKISTAN
SAUDI ARABIA
INDIA
MYANMAR
VIETNAM
LAOS
THAILAND
PHILIPPINES
ETHIOPIA
MALAYSIA
TANZANIA
AUSTRALIA
NEW ZEALAND

Where does Australia send foreign aid?

Australia focuses its foreign aid on the Asia-Pacific region.

$1.3 billion to Pacific nations

$1 billion to South-East Asia and East Asia

$290 million to South and West Asia

$260 million to the Middle East and Africa

$5.9 million to Latin America/ the Caribbean

What does Australia provide?

In total, Australia will provide $4.2 billion worth of aid in 2018–19. This represents less than 0.3 per cent of the nation's total income. To provide this aid, Australia partners with international financial institutions such as the World Bank, the United Nations, private sector companies, and non-governmental organisations

Australia's foreign aid includes:

1. **Helping** governments and communities be better prepared to respond in case of natural disasters.
2. **Preventing** the spread of infectious diseases with health programs.
3. **Funds** for United Nations organisations, the Red Cross and World Food Programme.
4. **Building** infrastructure, such as undersea telecommunications cables in Papua New Guinea and the Solomon Islands to improve internet connectivity.
5. **Training** security and law enforcement officials.

Cambodia

2018–19 OFFICIAL DEVELOPMENT ASSISTANCE:

$83.6 million

CAMBODIA HAS ONE of the lowest incomes per capita among South-East Asian countries. More than 13 per cent of the population lives below the poverty line, and although the economy is growing fast, the increasing wealth is not equally distributed.

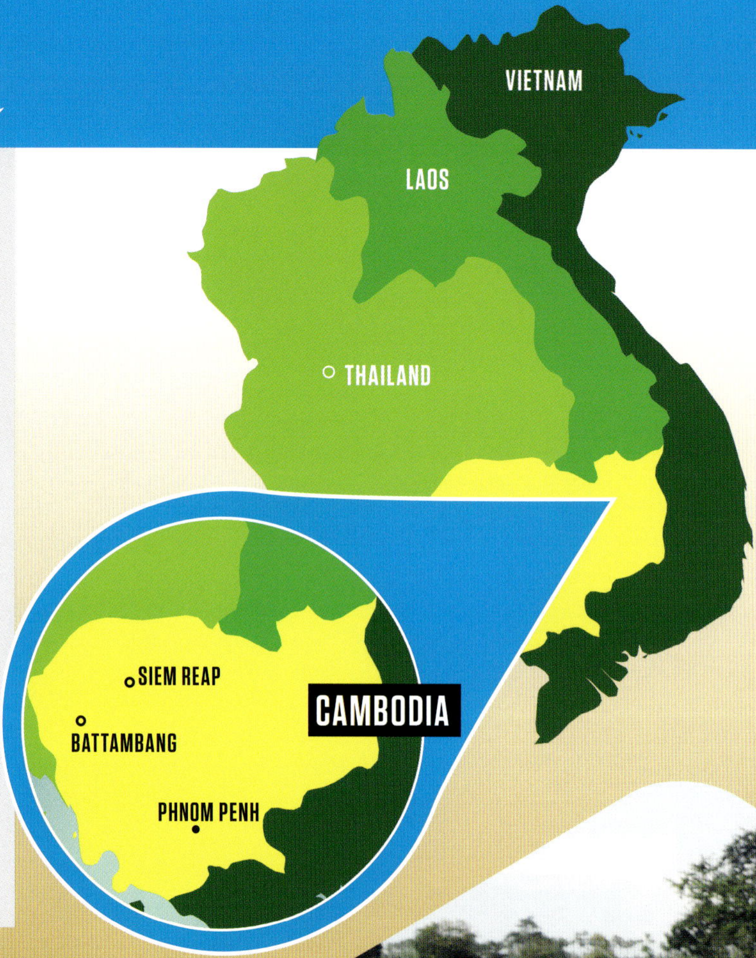

VIETNAM
LAOS
THAILAND
SIEM REAP
BATTAMBANG
PHNOM PENH
CAMBODIA

Australia's aid to Cambodia has three key objectives:

1. Improve infrastructure and access to basic transport, water and electricity services.
2. Boost agricultural productivity, especially rice yields.
3. Improve health and education.

Helping women

Australia's aid has a special focus on empowering women – for example helping them with healthcare during pregnancy and childbirth. The Ending Violence Against Women program aims to improve systems for women affected by domestic violence, and has helped more than 12,000 women and their families.

HEALTH OUTCOMES

The Health Equity Fund, supported by Australia, makes healthcare more affordable for the poorest Cambodians. In 2017, more than 2.64 million cases were subsidised by the Health Equity Fund. Australia also assists with disability services. However, Cambodia still faces significant health issues, such as the emergence of drug-resistant malaria.

CAMBODIAN AGRICULTURAL VALUE AID PROGRAM

Through this program, Australia has:

- **Helped to build relationships between farmers, suppliers, and retailers.**
- **Provided access to modern farming techniques.**
- **Improved farmers' crop quality and incomes.**
- **Cleared landmines to open up more land for agricultural use.**

Papua New Guinea

2018–19 OFFICIAL DEVELOPMENT ASSISTANCE:

$572.2 million

AUSTRALIA'S CLOSEST neighbor geographically, Papua New Guinea (PNG), is home to an incredible array of cultures, including hundreds of different Indigenous groups and more than 800 languages.

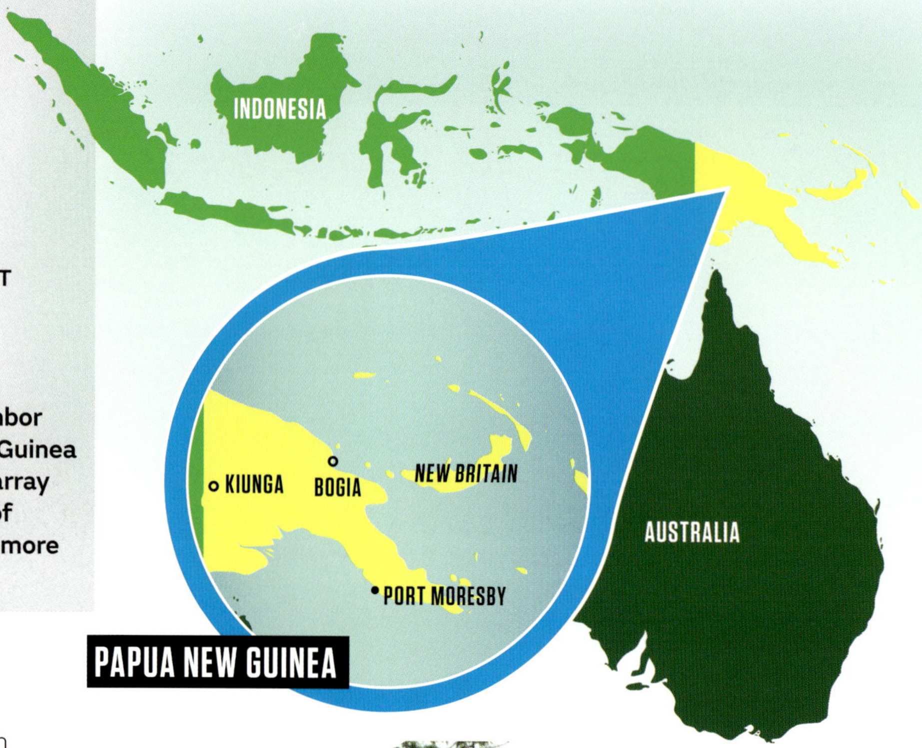

INDONESIA
KIUNGA
BOGIA
NEW BRITAIN
PORT MORESBY
AUSTRALIA
PAPUA NEW GUINEA

Although PNG is rich in natural resources, the majority of its population is very poor. The economic, educational and health challenges faced by PNG's people are serious. One in five children do not attend school, and an estimated 15 per cent of the population lives with disability.

PNG is also at risk of natural disasters including earthquake and volcanic eruption. Australia provided $5 million in humanitarian assistance following two major earthquakes in 2018.

Australia's aid to PNG has three key objectives:

Promoting effective governance: fair laws and non-corrupt government are essential for stability.

Enabling economic growth: engage with businesses, support infrastructure, upskilling of workers.

Enhancing human development: facilitating access to quality health services and education opportunities; training healthcare workers and teachers.

Across all three objectives, enhancing gender equality and empowering women is an important theme.

Did you know?

According to the DFAT, there are 10,000 Australians in Papua New Guinea at any given time.

INFRASTRUCTURE

- **Coral Sea Cable System** – providing internet access. Telecommunications is essential for economic growth and development, yet PNG has some of the poorest internet connectivity in the world. This undersea cable provides high-speed links between Australia, PNG and the Solomon Islands.
- **Road building and maintenance** – 1981km of road reconstructed or maintained in 2017.
- **Lighting Papua New Guinea** – less than 10% of PNG's population has access to the national electricity grid. This project provided more than 1.2 million people with solar lights.

Nepal

2018–19 OFFICIAL DEVELOPMENT ASSISTANCE:

$30.6 million

NEPAL IS AMONG the poorest countries in the world. Although Nepal has made progress in reducing poverty rates, many Nepalese people continue to face challenges, and in 2015, Nepal was struck by two destructive earthquakes that killed many people. The relationship between Nepal and Australia is strengthened through public and private contributions to economic and social development as well as tourism and migration.

Australia's aid to Nepal aims to:

1. Expand economic opportunities for the poor, especially women.
2. Support Nepal to improve its government.
3. Improve access to and quality of education.

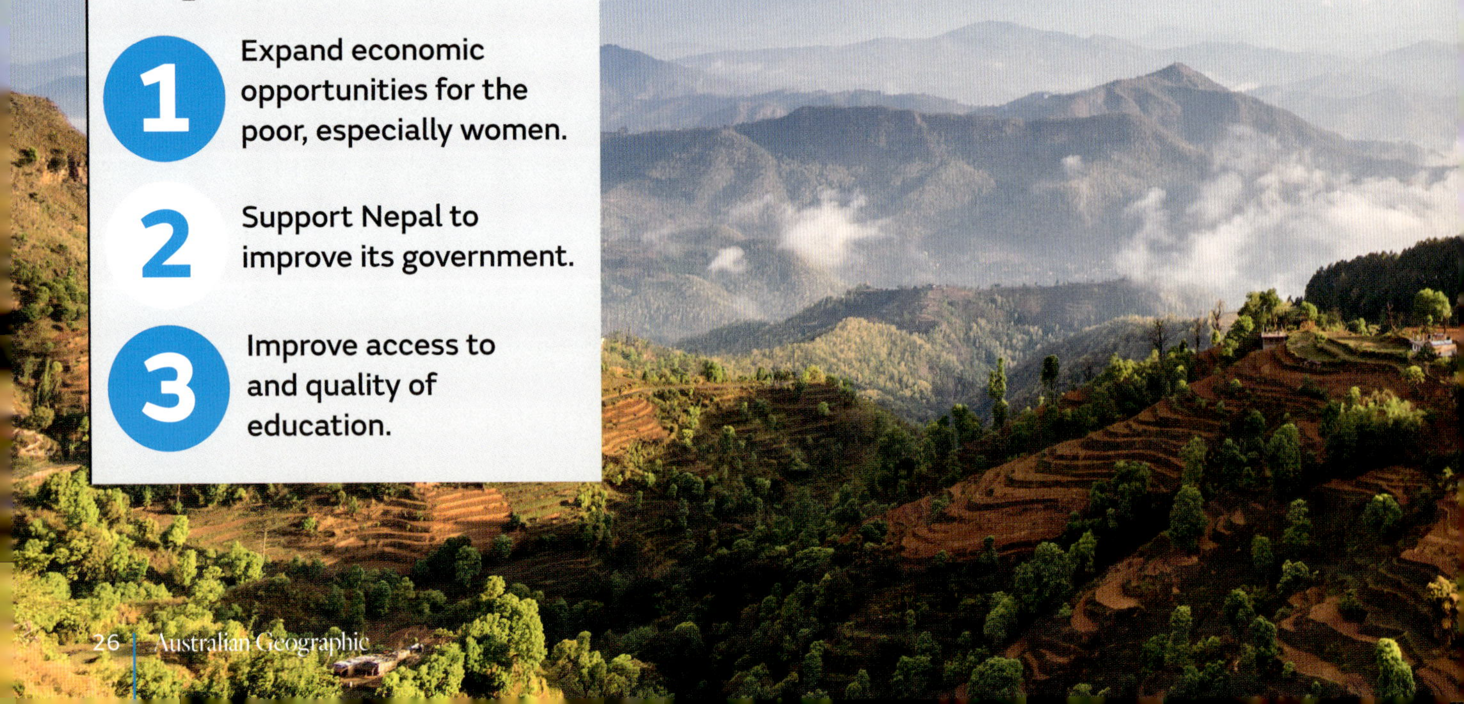

▲ Micro Enterprise Development Program
Led by the United Nations Development Program and funded by Australia, this project has created more than 195,000 jobs since 1998. The program assists the rural poor, women and other disadvantaged groups to develop entrepreneurial businesses, thereby helping to alleviate poverty.

▲ School Sector Reform Program
This program relates to Australia's objective of improving the quality of and access to education. Enrolment in primary education has increased from 73 per cent in 2009 to 91 per cent in 2016. Children's literacy rates (their ability to read) have also increased.

▲ 2015 Earthquakes
In 2015, two devastating earthquakes struck Nepal within the space of a few weeks, measuring 7.8 and 7.3 on the Richter scale. Approximately 9,000 people perished and about 20,000 were injured. Schools, roads, homes and other infrastructure were destroyed or damaged. Australia provided 15 tonnes of relief supplies and nearly $12 million worth of support through organisation such as Oxfam and the United Nations. Australia has subsequently given $16.7 million in recovery funds to help rebuild.

Vietnam

2018–19 OFFICIAL DEVELOPMENT ASSISTANCE:

$84.2 million

AUSTRALIA AND VIETNAM have a long-standing partnership, with Vietnamese people comprising the sixth largest migrant community in Australia. While Vietnam has experienced fast economic growth and no longer needs aid to subsidise basic services, fifteen million people in Vietnam still live below the national poverty line. Income inequality remains an issue, with ethnic minorities being more likely to live in poverty.

Promoting prosperity in Vietnam is important for stability in South-East Asia and ensuring Vietnam remains a strong trade partner for Australia. Australia's objectives for aid include:

1. Upskilling workforce and engaging private sector.
2. Alleviating poverty and gender inequality.
3. Promoting women's economic empowerment.

Results of the aid programs include access to clean water for 20,000 people, assisting farmers (with a strong focus on women farmers) to improve their techniques, and supporting more than 10,000 households in increasing their income.

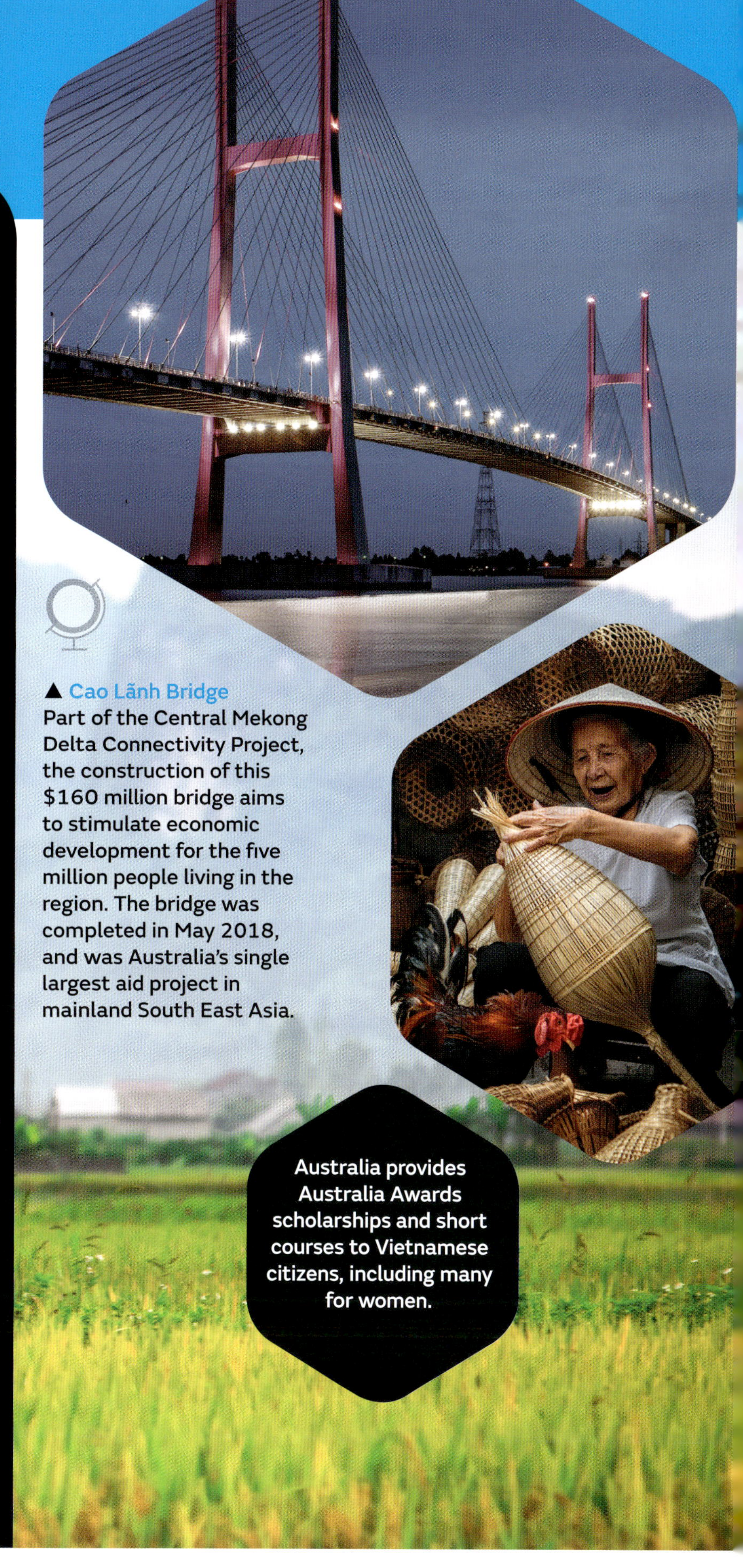

▲ Cao Lãnh Bridge
Part of the Central Mekong Delta Connectivity Project, the construction of this $160 million bridge aims to stimulate economic development for the five million people living in the region. The bridge was completed in May 2018, and was Australia's single largest aid project in mainland South East Asia.

Australia provides Australia Awards scholarships and short courses to Vietnamese citizens, including many for women.

Tonga

2018–19 OFFICIAL DEVELOPMENT ASSISTANCE:

$27.9 million

In Tonga, one-quarter of households struggle to meet their needs. The island nation is vulnerable to natural disasters and climate change, which in turn affects food security. Beyond aid, Australia is linked to Tonga through the Defence Cooperation Program, the Tonga Polica Development Program and through people. Approximately 25,000 Australians identify as having Tongan ancestry.

Pacific Women Shaping Pacific Development

This ten-year program, worth $320 million, aims to increase women's representation in Pacific governments, expand women's economic opportunities and reduce violence against women. Rates of domestic violence are high in Tonga, and this program aims to provide access to support services for women and families.

Natural disasters

Tonga is prone to natural disasters such as cyclones and earthquakes. Australia's aid has a focus on enhancing Tonga's disaster resilience and capacity to respond in emergencies.

Following Cyclone Gita in February 2018, Australia sent 135 tonnes of emergency supplies to Tonga and has contributed $14 million to the rebuild.

Australia has three priorities for aid in Tonga:

1. **Facilitating economic stability.**
2. **Reducing the burden of diseases such as diabetes and heart disease.**
3. **Supporting skill development and providing training opportunities.**

These are achieved through efforts to enhance preventative health services and access to disability services, and through programs such as the Pacific Labour Scheme. In this Scheme, workers from the Pacific region, including Tonga, can find employment in Australia in certain jobs. More than 10,000 Tongans have participated in the Scheme since 2008. Australia has supported Tonga to make important economic reforms, create smoke-free public spaces, and increase screening for diseases.

Image credits

Images are listed clockwise from top left.

Front cover: Ben Jeayes/Shutterstock (SS); DR Travel Photo and Video/SS; Nick Rains/Australian Geographic (AG); Phuong D. Nguyen/SS; Bill Bachman. **1:** Janaka Dharmasena/SS. **2:** Australian Geographic Cartography. **4:** Rodney Dekker/AG. **5:** Brian Cassey/AG; Brian Cassey/AG; PomInOz/SS; Brian Cassey/AG; Michael Amendolia/AG; Michael Amendolia/AG. **6:** Cathy Finch/AG. **8:** Avigator Fotuner/SS. **10:** IM_photo/SS; Cocos.Bounty/SS; ChameleonsEye/SS. **11:** Yuri Yavnik/SS; aphotostory/SS; Travel mania/SS. **12:** wolfpower/SS; Hampi/SS. **13:** Maurizio De Mattei/SS; Robert CGH. **14:** Riccardo Mayer/SS. **15:** Zzvet/SS; Juliya Shangarey/SS. **16:** pichitchai/SS; Adwo/SS. **17:** FiledIMAGE/SS; GTS Productions/SS; max blain/SS. **18:** Markus Mainka/SS; Heath Holden/AG. **19:** Lev Kropotov/SS; TonyNG/SS; Alf Manciagli/SS. **20:** Department of Foreign Affairs and Trade (DFAT)/Wikimedia Commons; DFAT/Wikimedia Commons; Dietmar Temps/SS. **21:** Pyty/SS. **22:** foo23/SS; Pyty/SS. **23:** Rawpixel.com/SS; Gil C/SS; Kevin Evans/AusAID/Wikimedia Commons; khlungcenter/SS; DFAT/Wikimedia Commons. **24:** N. Vector Design/SS; Pyty/SS; Francine Thompson/AusAID/Wikimedia Commons; Jacqueline Smart/AusAID/Wikimedia Commons; **25:** Silent O/SS; Rocky Roe/AusAID/Wikimedia Commons; Tetyana Dotsenko/SS. **26:** Thrithot/SS; Pyty/SS. **27:** noche/SS; My Good Images/SS; DFAT/Wikimedia Commons; Jim Holmes/AusAID/Wikimedia Commons. **28:** gnomeandi/SS; Pyty/SS; Gil C/SS; **29:** Bùi Thuy Đào Nguyên/Wikimedia Commons; TZIDO SUN/SS. **30:** NASA image created by Jesse Allen, Earth Observatory, using data obtained courtesy of the MODIS Rapid Response team/Wikimedia Commons; Pyty/SS; Scott McLennan/DFAT/Wikimedia Commons; Scott McLennan/DFAT/Wikimedia Commons; Loveshop/SS; **31:** Connor Ashleigh/AusAID/Wikimedia Commons; Connor Ashleigh/AusAID/Wikimedia Commons; Connor Ashleigh/AusAID/Wikimedia Commons; Scott McLennan/DFAT/Wikimedia Commons. **32:** Johan Swanepoel/SS. **Back cover:** Anton Balazh/SS.

First published in 2019 by:

Australian Geographic
54 Park Street, Sydney, NSW 2000
Telephone: (02) 9136 7214
Email: editorial@ausgeo.com.au

www.australiangeographic.com.au

Australian Geographic customer service:
1300 555 176 (local call rate within Australia).
From overseas +61 2 8667 5295

Funds from the sale of this book go to support the Australian Geographic Society, a not-for-profit organisation dedicated to sponsoring conservation and scientific projects, as well as adventures and expeditions.

Aboriginal and Torres Strait Islander people are advised that this book may contain images and names of people who have died.

Text Ellen Rykers and Australian Geographic contributors
Commercial Editor Lauren Smith
Assistant Commercial Editor Rebecca Cotton
Creative Director Mike Ellott
Designer Harmony Southern
Print Production Alisha Stoddart

Managing Director, Australian Geographic Jo Runciman
Editor-in-Chief, Australian Geographic Chrissie Goldrick